Savannah, Georgia, 1932

The smell of his grandma's biscuits lured Westley
to the kitchen. Westley was excited because today was
Thursday, the day he would see his mother. The rest of
the week, she worked for a white family just outside
Savannah, cooking, cleaning, and taking care of their
children. This was her day off.

Grandma's friend Old John was sitting at the table.
Westley loved listening to the old man's stories. Old
John had been born a slave. He had been taken from
his mother and had never known her. He was nine —
Westley's age — when he and all the slaves were freed
in 1865. Westley felt lucky — at least he saw his own
mama once a week.

Easter Shopping at Levy's

Once a year, sometime before Easter, Grandma would take Westley downtown to Levy's Department Store on Broughton Street to buy one nice outfit. They used a Levy's charge card and then paid a little bit each month.

On one shopping trip, the saleswoman would not serve them until after all the white customers had been helped. Westley had heard the saleswoman politely call the white women customers "Miss" and "Mrs." But she treated his grandma as if she were a child, a nobody.

Westley's grandma pretended not to notice. She was polite. But she was also proud. "Come on," she said, "it's time to go home." They left the store without buying a thing.

Segregation

Back then, black people weren't treated as well as white people. Most of the time, they were kept segregated from whites. Westley went to a separate school for black children. He had to drink from water fountains marked "Colored." He could not sit and eat at the Levy's lunch counter.

His Grandma's Prayers

Sometimes Westley got angry that black people were mistreated and that no matter how hard his mother worked, they were still poor. But his grandma was always there to talk with him. She understood why he was upset, but she didn't want him to have bad feelings about himself.

She said that no matter how he was treated, he had no excuse not to "be somebody." She told him again about the day he was born. She said, "I got on my knees and prayed that you would grow up to be a leader of our people."

Westley promised himself that he would fulfill his grandma's prayer. He also promised himself that he would work hard so that one day his mother would not have to work in someone else's house.

Voter Schools, 1942

Westley knew that many black people didn't vote because they had to pass a test to register. The test was designed to be difficult for black folk to pass. It was intended to keep them from voting.

Westley was a member of the Youth Council of the NAACP — the National Association for the Advancement of Colored People. The Youth Council started a special "voter school" in the basement of a church.

With his friend Clifford, Westley talked to everyone, even passersby, about voting. When he found someone who, scared by the test, had never registered to vote, he took them to the voter school. When they felt ready to take the test, Westley went with them to the courthouse and stayed until they were registered. With Westley's help and encouragement, many black people in Savannah became registered voters.

Working as a Mailman, 1949

After college and the army, Westley wanted to be a teacher. But because of his membership in the NAACP, no one in Savannah would hire him.

So Westley became a mailman. The postal service hired qualified people, regardless of their color. As it turned out, this job suited Westley just fine.

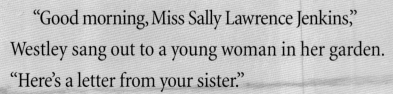

"Good morning, Miss Sally Lawrence Jenkins," Westley sang out to a young woman in her garden. "Here's a letter from your sister."

Westley liked to address people by their full names. He could trace a person's history in their name. And history was important to Westley. "If you don't know where you've been, how do you know where you're going?" he loved to ask.

At the NAACP Office
February 1960

After work, Westley spent long evenings at the NAACP office. One night, he was visited by a group of students who were excited about what was happening in Greensboro, North Carolina. Young black people there had staged a sit-in at a lunch counter in a local store. They had refused to leave until they were served.

The students standing in front of Westley wanted to do the same thing at the department stores on Broughton Street. But they needed a leader. Westley remembered how his grandma had been treated at Levy's, and he agreed to help. But first, the students had to be trained. They had to protest without ever using violence, even if the other side did. If they were attacked and they fought back, Westley told them, their cause would be lost.

Levy's Lunch Counter

After weeks of training, small groups of students made their way downtown, entered the big stores along Broughton Street, and sat down at the lunch counters. The stores refused to serve them. At Levy's, the manager called the police, who arrested the students for breaking the city's segregation laws.

Throwing Down Their Cards

Westley called a mass meeting the next Sunday at the Bolton Street Baptist Church. People filled the pews and balconies. Westley opened the meeting with a hymn. All the voices singing together made a thunderous sound. And the mighty noise made people think that perhaps working together, they could really make something happen. Westley spoke about the arrests of the young people at Levy's. He said that things had to change, and he asked if people were ready to fight for their rights.

Someone shouted, "I'll never shop at that store again!" Then someone in the balcony threw down a Levy's charge card. Soon, everyone was tossing charge cards into a big pile in the church.

The Boycott Begins
March 17, 1960

The next morning, Westley led a group downtown. They carried baskets full of charge cards.

At Levy's, Westley and his group dumped the baskets of charge cards onto the sidewalk. Then Westley announced that no black people would shop at any store on Broughton Street until they were treated equally.

The Great Savannah Boycott had begun!

Picket Lines

Westley and other members of the NAACP organized a picket line every day in front of Levy's. White people yelled and jeered at the protesters and tried to force them off the sidewalk. But day after day, the protesters returned.

One day a large, burly white man punched one of the demonstrators in the face and broke his jaw. But everyone remembered what Westley had taught them. They didn't yell or fight back, no matter how much they wanted to.

Westley organized other protests. There were kneel-ins at the white churches on Sundays and wade-ins at the all-white beach at Tybee. Westley wanted to end segregation everywhere in Savannah — in libraries, theaters, public pools, beaches, and restrooms, as well as at lunch counters.

Talking About Peaceful Change

Large meetings were held every Sunday at different churches. Protesters talked about their activities; some gave fiery speeches. The meetings became so popular that no church was big enough to hold everyone who wanted to get in.

For a year and a half, no one from the black community shopped on Broughton Street.

Westley walked down the street and started counting: One, two, three, four, five GOING OUT OF BUSINESS signs. The white storeowners couldn't stay in business without black customers.

When he delivered mail to white people, Westley told them how much he loved Savannah. He wanted the city to be a better place for everyone. They respected Westley. They saw how peaceful and committed to change the protesters were. Little by little, more and more white people began to sympathize with the protesters.

Desegregation Without Violence

White people in the community who supported Westley asked what they could do to end segregation and stop the boycott. Together, leaders from the white and black communities worked out a plan. Each evening after delivering the mail, Westley organized a group of students to sit in at a different kind of business or facility the next day. The theaters would be first, then the restaurants, then the library, and on down the line until every business had been desegregated.

Sometimes angry crowds would gather, or white people would leave in protest when the black students arrived. But most of the white and black leaders stuck together. The mayor made sure that all the signs marking separate facilities for blacks and whites at City Hall, the courthouse, health department, and hospital were taken down. City officials took the segregation laws off the books. Unlike desegregation efforts in other cities and towns in the South, there was very little violence in Savannah.

Justice Delivered

On a Sunday in September 1961, Westley greeted the hundreds of people who arrived at a downtown Savannah church. Inside, their voices joined together to sing out, "We are Soldiers in God's Army." When the song ended, Westley stood in front of the crowd. He saw his mother sitting in the front row. He saw students who had been arrested. He saw faces beaming with pride. Then he announced in a loud clear voice, "We have triumphed!"

Savannah was the first southern city in the United States to declare all its citizens equal, three years before the federal Civil Rights Act made all segregation illegal. People, both black and white, saw Westley as Savannah's hero. He had kept the protest disciplined and peaceful, even in the face of violence. Modestly, he would say, "I was just doing what every black American should be doing."

Westley Wallace Law delivered more than just the mail to the citizens of Savannah; he delivered justice, too. His grandma's prayers had been answered.

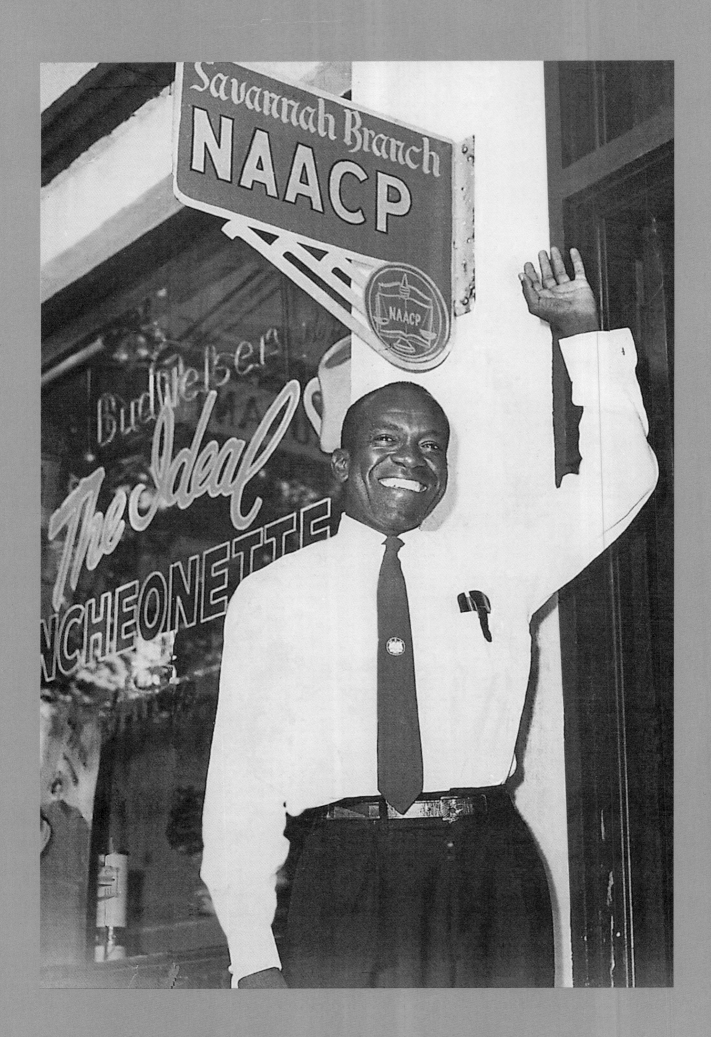

Afterword

Until his death at the age of seventy-nine, on July 29, 2002, Westley Wallace Law, known to most as W.W., continued to fulfill his grandma's prayers. He worked tirelessly to end racial discrimination and to fight for justice.

In September 1961, during the final days of the boycott, W.W. was fired from his job as a letter carrier when U.S. Representative G. Elliott Hagan made him a campaign issue. Hagan promised to get rid of the "troublemaker from the NAACP." But in October, President John F. Kennedy came to his defense, and W.W. was reinstated with back pay. He continued to work as a mailman for forty-two years.

He served on the national board of directors of the NAACP for thirty years. And he served as president of the Georgia Branch of the NAACP for thirteen years. He faced intimidation and death threats. Medgar Evers, an NAACP field secretary, was murdered outside his home in Mississippi in June 1963. W.W. narrowly escaped an attempt on his own life when the NAACP offices in Savannah were attacked. He said he could never marry or have children because it would be too dangerous.

Ever since W.W. had been a young boy listening to the stories of his elders, he believed in the importance of history. Preserving and teaching history to young people became his crusade. In the 1970s, he began a project restoring gravesites at Laurel Grove South Cemetery, a predominantly black cemetery in Savannah. He founded the Savannah-Yamacraw Branch of the Association for the Study of Afro-American Life and History and created the Negro Heritage Trail tour of historic Savannah. He organized the Beach Institute Historic Neighborhood to preserve Savannah's only remaining downtown black neighborhood and to prevent black displacement from the inner city. He spearheaded efforts to restore the King-Tisdell Cottage and Beach Institute.

In February 1996, W.W. was chosen as the only Savannahian to have his likeness included in the mural on the Atlanta Centennial Olympic Wall. It was because of W.W.'s vision that the Ralph Mark Gilbert Civil Rights Museum in Savannah was established.

Among the awards W.W. received, many were for his work as a preservationist. He was awarded the Historic Savannah Foundation's Davenport Award, the first black Savannahian to receive the honor; the Distinguished Georgian Award by the Center for the Study of Georgia History; and the National Preservation Award by the National Trust for Historic Preservation for lifetime achievement. He was also awarded the highest honor from the Georgia Trust for Historic Preservation as "a pioneer in African American historic preservation efforts in Georgia and a dynamic leader in Savannah."

He never took money for the public service work that he did, choosing to live on the small wages he earned from the United States Postal Service. He wanted to live as an ordinary citizen and teach by example. Living frugally, never owning a car, never buying fancy things, he was able to fulfill his lifelong dream. He sat his mother down one day and told her that she did not have to go live and work in someone else's house anymore. She could finally stay home in the house he had bought for her.

To all who have walked with W. W. Law throughout
his crusade in life, and to those who are yet to come: let us
pick up the torch and live the legacy that he passes on.

W.W. Law photograph opposite afterword courtesy of *Savannah Morning News*

Design Press is a division of the Savannah College of Art and Design.

First edition 2005

Library of Congress Cataloging-in-Publication Data

Haskins, James, date.
Delivering justice : W.W. Law and the fight for civil rights / Jim Haskins ; illustrated by Benny Andrews. — 1st ed.
p.   cm.
ISBN 0-7636-2592-2
1. Law, W.W. (Westley Wallace), 1923–2002 — Juvenile literature. 2. African American civil rights workers — Georgia —
Savannah — Biography — Juvenile literature. 3. Civil rights workers — Georgia — Savannah — Biography — Juvenile literature.
4. African Americans — Civil rights — Georgia — Savannah — History — 20th century — Juvenile literature.
5. Civil rights movements — Georgia — Savannah — History — 20th century — Juvenile literature.
6. Savannah (Ga.) — Race relations — Juvenile literature. 7. Savannah (Ga.) — Biography — Juvenile literature.
I. Andrews, Benny, date. ill. II. Title.

F294.S2H24 2005
323'.092 — dc22   2005047114

2 4 6 8 10 9 7 5 3

Printed in China

This book is typeset in Minion Condensed.
The illustrations were done in oil and collage on paper.

Candlewick Press
2067 Massachusetts Avenue
Cambridge, Massachusetts 02140

visit us at www.candlewick.com